Change Your Mindset Change Your Life

Create the Foundation for Developing New Habits for a
Lifetime of Success and Happiness

Passionate for Life, Gainesville FL, USA

Change Your Mindset Change Your Life: Create the Foundation for Developing New Habits for a Lifetime of Success and Happiness

Published in the United States by Passionate for Life, Gainesville, FL.

ISBN-13: 978-1530229758

www.angeliquebochnak.com

Photo Credits: Unsplash.com, free (do whatever you want with) high-resolution photos.
Cover Design by CreativWriter at www.creativwriter.com

Limits of Liability and Disclaimer Warranty
The author shall not be liable for your misuse of this material. This book is strictly for informational and educational purposes.

Printed in the United States of America

FREE DOWNLOAD

Get a FREE printable pdf companion book.

Guided Motivation: Guidebook for Self-Reflection, Journal Your way to Success and Happiness is the perfect companion for this book.

Sign up for author's New Releases mailing list and get a FREE companion workbook.

Click here to get started: http://eepurl.com/bRBdhb

Also by Angelique Bochnak:

Guided Motivation: Guidebook for Self-Reflection, Journal Your way to Success and Happiness

Contents

Dedicated to Sara for always believing in me and encouraging me to follow my dreams

How to use this book...

Every year countless people set goals. Especially at the start of a New Year. Most of us will come up with at least a few things we want to accomplish or change in the upcoming year. Unfortunately too many of us forget about them within a month. Are you one of those people?

Setting goals is a great thing. Maybe you desire to lose weight, get a new job, pay off your credit card debt, go back to college, buy a house, or start a family. These are all great goals. Unfortunately, year after year, too many goals just like these go unmet. Why? Why do we do this to ourselves? Over and over again, we set ourselves up for disappointment and failure. I am guilty of setting goals and then forgetting about them, losing focus and falling into my old habits. Are you?

How can we change this bad pattern? Let's talk about habits! Your habits are the key to changing your life. If you have goals you keep setting for yourself that you can never seem to achieve, maybe you need to take a long, hard look at your habits.

Your habits, in many respects, define your potential for success. If you are someone with a lot of bad habits, then meeting goals and creating change in your life will be difficult. Whereas if you already have some good habits and you still can't reach those goals, then it's time to look closer at your discipline and focus.

Before you can begin to evaluate your habits, you have a critical decision to make. If you want to actually meet your goals and create positive change in your life, you have to decide you want to change your habits. More importantly, you have to know what habits you need to change. Achieving goals only comes with change. You have to want to change. Let me say that again. YOU HAVE TO WANT TO CHANGE.

It's not enough to just say you want to change. You have to feel it, embody it, and then live it. True life-impacting change that sets you on a new path of discovery, success, and happiness is almost spiritual. That might sound kooky to some of you, but is true. Once you realize this for yourself, your positive change will happen.

Change is hard. Any kind of change is never easy. We are creatures of habit. We get into a regular schedule and we do not like it when that schedule is disrupted. It is not in our nature to change. With change comes new habits. New habits replace old habits. Old habits are hard to break.

Before change can occur, you first have to identify
1) What you don't like about your current situation and why?;
2) What you want out of life and why?;
3) What bad habits are holding you back?
4) What new habits you need to replace the old habits;
5) What is your motivation and how do you find it?;
6) Discipline yourself; and
7) Focus.

You will notice in items 1 and 2, you are asked to identify the 'why.' The 'why' is important. If you do not identify why you are unhappy or why you want the things you want, it will make it harder for you to work for that change. Defining your 'why' is a very powerful tool. Once you define why you need change and why you want the things you want, it becomes easier to define your vision for your future. Your vision is what you see for yourself and your family.

Where do you want to go?
Where is your ideal place to live?
What is your ideal image?
What is your ideal weight?
What is your ideal job?
What does your dream house look like?

These are all questions that can be addressed in your vision. Your 'why' will help you narrow in on your vision. Never lose focus of your "why."

This book is divided into six sections:
- Prep Work
- Week 1: Define Your Habits
- Week 2: Find Your Motivation
- Week 3: The Power of Discipline
- Week 4: Feed Your Focus
- What Next?

Each of these sections contain critical steps and activities that you need to evaluate before you can expect positive change to occur in your life. Depending on where you are in your personal journey will determine how critical each activity is or which ones will be the most helpful. Regardless, I encourage you to take each section seriously and go through each of the steps. The more thorough you are with this process the greater your chances of success.

Now let's jump into each of these sections and start creating life-impacting change.

Prep Work

Day 1

Day 2

Prep Work

This is a critical step. Do not skip this step. You will spend two days seriously reflecting on your life, your past, and your future. These two days are the only two days you should think about your past. After these two days, you need to let your past go. It's exactly that, your past. Hanging onto your past will only keep you from reaching your future.

> *"The privilege of a lifetime is being who you are."*
> –Joseph Campbell

This is your self-discovery phase. Planning and setting goals is a critical process in achieving success. But before you can expect to set goals and actually achieve them, you must reflect on who you are and where you want to go first. This phase is the backbone of this four week process of changing your mindset so that you can change your life. So take it serious. We will talk about long-term goal setting more under the What Next? section.

Having awareness of your negative thoughts is the first step to transforming your life. If you truly want to improve the quality of your life, you need to write down, analyze, and overcome your negative thoughts. The problem is these negative thoughts have become habitual. Don't be too hard on yourself but be honest. We will deal with your bad habits that may be driven by your negative thoughts during week 1.

I stumbled across this process somewhat by accident. I was in search of a good day planner and instead found a life coach disguised as a day planner. In many respects this planner was a typical planner, but it had all these interesting questions incorporated throughout it. I found myself skipping all the way to the end just to get through these critical questions.

This prep work was critical for me to realize my dream of writing. I did not fully realize what I wanted to do with my career until I went through this process. Nor did I understand what was holding me back or my definition of success. Once these things were clear to me, I was able to define my life vision and course out a plan to make it happen.

I have summarized the process I discovered into the following two days of self-reflection. The questioned included are the questions that were the most important to my life-impacting change. I hope you will take these questions seriously and take the time necessary to reflect on your life.

For many of you, Day 1 and Day 2 may take longer than any other day in this process. It's ok if you take longer than two days to address all the questions in Day 1 and write your vision in Day 2. It's more important to get it done, and to get it done right, than it is to get it done fast. Change takes time, don't rush this process. Nothing great happens overnight.

If there is not enough space to write your responses in the pages provided, feel free to grab a notebook or journal. Write as much as you need. This is your journey.

Day 1: Reflection for Self-Discovery
Day 2: Define Your Vision

Day 1: Reflection for Self-Discovery

1. List at least 3 things you would like to change about your job. Why?

_____

_____

_____

_____

_____

_____

_____

2. List 3 things you would like to change about your personal life. Why?

_____

_____

_____

_____

_____

_____

_____

3. List 3 things you would like to change about yourself. Why?

_____

_____

_____

_____

_____

_____

_____

4. Would you describe yourself as "generally happy" or "generally unhappy"? Why?

_____

_____

_____

_____

_____

Day 1: Self-Discovery (continued)

1. What is most important to you in life?

   _____

   _____

   _____

   _____

2. What are your top 3 strengths?

   _____

   _____

   _____

3. What lights you up? List your passions.

   _____

   _____

   _____

   _____

4. If money or education were not an issue, what would you love to do for a living?

   _____

   _____

   _____

   _____

5. What weaknesses do you need to work on?

   _____

   _____

   _____

   _____

6. How do you define success? What does a successful life look like to you?

   _____

   _____

   _____

   _____

Day 1: Self-Discovery (continued)

Write down the first thing that come to mind as it relates to you and where you are in your life today for each of the following thoughts. Don't over think, just write down your immediate thoughts.

Thought	Your Response
I am not good enough for that	
I am worthy of love and respect	
I am not smart enough to learn that	
I can do anything I set my mind to	
I would like to do that, but I am afraid	
I am afraid, but I am going to do it anyway	
I am too old/young to do or learn that now	
No matter what the obstacle, I will succeed	

Day 2: Define Your Vision

1. Describe your perfect life as if it were happening right now. What would you like to feel like? What would you like to be doing? What experiences would you like to have?

   _____

   _____

   _____

   _____

   _____

   _____

   _____

   _____

2. Describe your ideal environment. Where would you be living? What would it smell like, look like, and sound like?

   _____

   _____

   _____

   _____

   _____

   _____

   _____

   _____

3. Describe your morals, values, and unique qualities that make you who you are or what you want to become. Do you see yourself as a leader, innovator, a person living in a small town with a family, simple life, or big city life?

   _____

   _____

   _____

   _____

   _____

   _____

Day 2: Define Your Vision (continued)

Use your responses to the previous questions to formulate your vision. What do you want out of life? Describe your ideal life. Identify the things you want in life, both intangible and tangible. Be Specific. Include all areas of your life.

_____

_____

_____

_____

_____

_____

_____

_____

_____

_____

_____

_____

_____

_____

_____

_____

_____

_____

_____

_____

_____

_____

_____

_____

_____

_____

_____

_____

_____

_____

Week 1:

**Examine
Your Habits**

Day 3

Day 4

Day 5

Day 6

Day 7

Day 8

Day 9

Week 1: Define your Habits

Now that you have defined what you want for your life, it's time to learn how to make it a reality. Let's tackle some bad habits that may be holding you back. Without realizing it, you may have several bad habits that are keeping you from achieving the level of success you desire and deserve. Most of you may never have given your habits any thought. You may not even realize that some of the things you do regularly have become habits. These habits are hard to break.

> *"Bad habits are easy to form, but hard to live with.*
> *Good habits are hard to form, but easy to live with.*
> *Everything is hard before it's easy."*
> –Brian Tracy

Here is a simple example:

> A recent habit that I changed in my life was dessert after dinner. I needed to lose a lot of weight and I finally made the decision to make that change over a year ago. The first thing to go was dessert after dinner every single night. It had become a habit for me and my family. It was an expected daily event. Unfortunately I seemed to be the only one seriously affected by that habit. I gained so much weight. But through self-reflection and discovery, I set out to change my daily habits with regards to eating food. I also knew that in order for me to have success in weight loss, my family had to join me on this journey. So bye, bye dessert. It was hard on everybody at first. But after a couple of weeks, everyone began to get used to the new schedule. Dessert was now something we only had once per week. We replaced a bad habit with a better habit. I took it a step further and only have dessert once a month. That's a good habit. As a result, I was able to create positive change for my health.

See how this works? Great!

Now let's identify some of your bad habits and good habits. Think about Day 1 and Day 2 and the things you identified through your self-discovery and vision. Think about the habits you have that may be holding you back. You will spend each day of this week accomplishing the following tasks:

- Day 3, you will define your bad habits;
- Day 4 you will define your good habits;
- Day 5 you will identify new habits you need to enforce that will help you achieve your vision; and
- Days 6 through 9 you will focus on how to enforce these new habits into your life.

Keep in mind, it takes a lot longer than a few days to create permanent new habits. It could take anywhere from a few weeks to several months to reach the point where these new actions become permanent habits. This process, however, will help you establish the foundation required to create permanent change in your life.

Day 3: Define existing bad habits
Day 4: Define existing good habits
Day 5: Identify New habits
Day 6: Solidify New Habits
Day 7: Solidify New Habits
Day 8: Solidify New Habits
Day 9: Solidify New Habits

Day 3: Define Existing Bad Habits

List every bad habit you can think of that may be holding you back. These habits could be as simple as chatting with colleagues every morning before beginning your work day, buying drive-through breakfast, smoking, eating unhealthy snacks, surfing the internet, or playing on your smart phone. You know your bad habits that hinder your productivity. Write them down and describe why they are bad for you.

_____
_____
_____
_____
_____
_____
_____
_____
_____
_____
_____
_____
_____
_____
_____
_____
_____
_____
_____
_____
_____
_____
_____
_____
_____
_____

Day 4: Define Existing Good Habits

List every good habit you can think of that will help you achieve success in reaching your goals. Good habits could be as simple as getting up early to plan your day, eating a healthy breakfast, exercising, reading, schedule email and internet time or avoiding office gossip. Write them down and describe why they are good for you.

_____

_____

_____

_____

_____

_____

_____

_____

_____

_____

_____

_____

_____

_____

_____

_____

_____

_____

_____

_____

_____

_____

_____

_____

_____

_____

_____

Day 5: Identify New Habits

Now we start to have fun. This is where you get to do a bit of research. There are lots of websites that describe habits of successful people. I suggest you do an internet search for 'good habits for success' and read a few of articles. Since every person is different and every person's vision is going to be unique to them, I have found it isn't easy to simply apply a blanket list of good habits to everyone. After you read a few web articles, pick 3 or 4 habits that you feel will help you achieve your goals and write them down. Why?

_____

_____

_____

_____

_____

_____

_____

_____

_____

_____

_____

_____

_____

_____

_____

_____

_____

_____

_____

_____

_____

_____

_____

_____

Day 6: Solidify New Habits

Write down each of the habits you identified yesterday and describe what you will do to make sure you work on them.

Habit 1_____
How will you make sure you do this habit today?

_____

_____

_____

_____

_____

Habit 2_____
How will you make sure you do this habit today?

_____

_____

_____

_____

_____

Habit 3_____
How will you make sure you do this habit today?

_____

_____

_____

_____

_____

Habit 4_____
How will you make sure you do this habit today?

_____

_____

_____

_____

_____

Day 7: Solidify New Habits

Habit 1_____

Did you implement this habit yesterday? YES or NO

If yes, great. Keep it up. If no, what could you do differently today to make sure you do?

_____

_____

_____

Habit 2_____

Did you implement this habit yesterday? YES or NO

If yes, great. Keep it up. If no, what could you do differently today to make sure you do?

_____

_____

_____

Habit 3_____

Did you implement this habit yesterday? YES or NO

If yes, great. Keep it up. If no, what could you do differently today to make sure you do?

_____

_____

_____

Habit 4_____

Did you implement this habit yesterday? YES or NO

If yes, great. Keep it up. If no, what could you do differently today to make sure you do?

_____

_____

_____

Day 8: Solidify New Habits

Habit 1_____

Did you implement this habit yesterday? YES or NO

If yes, great. Keep it up. If no, what could you do differently today to make sure you do?

_____

_____

_____

Habit 2_____

Did you implement this habit yesterday? YES or NO

If yes, great. Keep it up. If no, what could you do differently today to make sure you do?

_____

_____

_____

Habit 3_____

Did you implement this habit yesterday? YES or NO

If yes, great. Keep it up. If no, what could you do differently today to make sure you do?

_____

_____

_____

Habit 4_____

Did you implement this habit yesterday? YES or NO

If yes, great. Keep it up. If no, what could you do differently today to make sure you do?

_____

_____

_____

Day 9: Solidify New Habits

Habit 1_____

Did you implement this habit yesterday? YES or NO

If yes, great. Keep it up. If no, what could you do differently today to make sure you do?

_____

_____

_____

Habit 2_____

Did you implement this habit yesterday? YES or NO

If yes, great. Keep it up. If no, what could you do differently today to make sure you do?

_____

_____

_____

Habit 3_____

Did you implement this habit yesterday? YES or NO

If yes, great. Keep it up. If no, what could you do differently today to make sure you do?

_____

_____

_____

Habit 4_____

Did you implement this habit yesterday? YES or NO

If yes, great. Keep it up. If no, what could you do differently today to make sure you do?

_____

_____

_____

Week 2: Find Your Motivation

What motivates you?

This is my favorite step in the process. I am easily inspired by beautiful quotes and images. When I realized this about myself, it became easy for me to create change in my life. So much so, I now start every single day reading quotes. I read at least 4 quotes a morning and reflect on how each quote makes me feel. It only takes about 10-15 minutes. I do it while I am drinking my morning coffee before anyone else in the house gets up. This way it is quite and my mind is free to think without distraction.

> *"It is not in the stars to hold our destiny but in ourselves."*
> —William Shakespeare

During week 2 you will use quotes to reflect on your life. Days 10 through 13 will be guided motivation. On these four days, you are provided with 4 quotes each day. Read these quotes and write down how each of them make you feel. Do they make you feel happy or inspired? Do they make you smile? Do they make you want to get up and do something? If yes, what? Write down whatever you feel.

On days 14 through 16, you are going to practice self-motivation. On these three days you are responsible for looking up and writing down you're your own quotes and reflect on how they make you feel. Same process, but you need to find quotes that inspire you.

There are lots of website and blogs that center solely around quotes. Do an internet search on quotes to inspire and you will find more than enough. I have also created a book on this process called *Guided Motivation: Guidebook for Self-Reflection, Journal Your way to Success and Happiness*. You can buy a copy on www.amazon.com or sign up for my email list at this link to receive a free, printable pdf version: http://eepurl.com/bRBdhb

In addition to reflecting on quotes, each day you will still have a small section at the bottom to solidify new habits. This section is called "Habit Check." Use this space to reflect on the same questions you were asked on Days 6 through 9. You can't forget about those new habits. Long-lasting change will not happen without them.

Day 10: Guided Motivation
Day 11: Guided Motivation
Day 12: Guided Motivation
Day 13: Guided Motivation
Day 14: Self-Motivation
Day 15: Self-Motivation
Day 16: Self-Motivation

Day 10: Guided Motivation

"Hope never abandons you, you abandon it." – George Weinberg

_____
_____
_____
_____
_____

"When was the last time you did something for the first time?" -- Unknown

_____
_____
_____
_____
_____

"Life isn't about finding yourself. Life is about creating yourself." – George Bernard Shaw

_____
_____
_____
_____
_____

"I always had a repulsive need to be something more than human." – David Bowie

_____
_____
_____
_____
_____

Habit Check?
Habit 1:
Habit 2:
Habit 3:
Habit 4:

Day 11: Guided Motivation

"You're a different human being to everybody you meet." – Chuck
Palahniuk

_____

_____

_____

_____

_____

"I need a life that isn't just about needing to escape my life." – Roberto
Polito

_____

_____

_____

_____

_____

"I am in competition with myself and I'm losing." – Roger Walters

_____

_____

_____

_____

_____

"What a tremendous thing to believe a person is more than a person."
– John Green

_____

_____

_____

_____

_____

Habit Check?
Habit 1:
Habit 2:
Habit 3:
Habit 4:

Day 12: Guided Motivation

"Be yourself, everyone else is already taken." – Oscar Wilde

_____

_____

_____

_____

_____

"Don't cry because it's over, smile because it happened." – Dr. Seuss

_____

_____

_____

_____

_____

"There are only two ways to live your life. One is as though nothing is a miracle. The other is as though everything is a miracle." – Albert Einstein

_____

_____

_____

_____

_____

"In three words I can sum up everything I've learned about life: it goes on." – Robert Frost

_____

_____

_____

_____

_____

Habit Check?
Habit 1:
Habit 2:
Habit 3:
Habit 4:

Day 13: Guided Motivation

"Insanity is doing the same thing, over and over again, but expecting a different result." – Narcotics Anonymous

_____

_____

_____

_____

"To be yourself in a world that is constantly trying to make you something else is the greatest accomplishment." – Ralph Waldo Emerson

_____

_____

_____

_____

_____

"Life is what happens to you when you are busy making other plans." – Allen Saunders

_____

_____

_____

_____

_____

"You only live once, but if you do it right, once is enough." – Mae West

_____

_____

_____

_____

_____

Habit Check?
Habit 1:
Habit 2:
Habit 3:
Habit 4:

Day 14: Self-Motivation

Quote:

_____

_____

Reflection:

_____

_____

Quote:

_____

_____

Reflection:

_____

_____

Quote:

_____

_____

Reflection:

_____

_____

Quote:

_____

_____

Reflection:

_____

_____

Habit Check?	
Habit 1:	
Habit 2:	
Habit 3:	
Habit 4:	

Day 15: Self-Motivation

Quote:

_____

_____

Reflection:

_____

_____

Quote:

_____

_____

Reflection:

_____

_____

Quote:

_____

_____

Reflection:

_____

_____

Quote:

_____

_____

Reflection:

_____

_____

Habit Check?
Habit 1:
Habit 2:
Habit 3:
Habit 4:

Day 16: Self-Motivation

Quote:

_____

_____

Reflection:

_____

_____

Quote:

_____

_____

Reflection:

_____

_____

Quote:

_____

_____

Reflection:

_____

_____

Quote:

_____

_____

Reflection:

_____

_____

Habit Check?
Habit 1:
Habit 2:
Habit 3:
Habit 4:

Week 3: The Power of Discipline

Without discipline, you will never obtain the level of success you deserve. If you have made it to week three, congratulations. You have already proven you have what it takes to discipline yourself to change your life. Change not only takes desire, it takes discipline.

> *"You can achieve almost any goal you set for yourself*
> *if you have the discipline to pay the price,*
> *to do what you need to do,*
> *and to never give up."*
> –Brian Tracy

In week 3, you will continue to reinforce your new habits, motivate yourself, and strengthen your foundation for change. By this point, you should be ready to commit to a real change in your life. You should already be disciplining yourself to let this change happen.

You have already completed one of the most difficult steps in this process, critiquing yourself. But now is when things begin to get hard. Real change takes discipline and consistency. If you want to create permanency with your new habits, then you need to have discipline and be consistent.

Consistency is the number one reason I have seen people fail. It's not good enough to do something one day and then forget about for three or four days. You can't have one great week and then slack off for a couple of weeks and still expect to achieve your goals. You need to learn to discipline yourself to be consistent. Think of these actions as non-negotiables. Do or die, you will get your non-negotiables accomplished every single day.

A great example of a non-negotiable is reinforcing your new habits that you worked on last week. By making it a priority to work on new, good habits every single day, you are making that a non-negotiable.

Now let's take it a step further and really test your discipline. This week you will be ask to create daily challenges. These challenge exercises are meant to be completed in a single day. They should be short challenges that do not require a lot of time. Consider this practice for your future and a test of your will. But it needs to be something that will be challenging for you to complete. Otherwise it's not a challenge.

An example would be not drinking coffee for one day. This challenge would be hard for many people, myself included. The point is to prove to yourself that you have the discipline it takes to make a change, no matter how small or short term.

You will also notice that each day still includes your Habit Check and your Daily Self-Motivation. All we are doing is building onto this process with each week making you stronger and closer to change.

Day 17: It takes Discipline
Day 18: Growing the foundation
Day 19: Reinforcing the foundation
Day 20: Accept No Excuses, Daily Challenge #1
Day 21: Daily Challenge #2
Day 22: Daily Challenge #3
Day 23: Daily Challenge #4

Day 17: It Takes Discipline

Self-discipline is the number one trait needed to accomplish goals. Hopefully you have taken the first two weeks of this journey seriously and you have already begun creating the habits necessary for a self-disciplined person. If yes, then you have already begun building a strong foundation. Today, I want you to make a list of at least 10 goals you would like to achieve in the next year. Write them down no matter how big or small.

1._____
2._____
3._____
4._____
5._____
6._____
7._____
8._____
9._____
10._____

Now evaluate each of the new good habits you have been working on each day. Do those new habits help you achieve all or most of these goals? If yes, how? If no, what habits do you need to change?

_____
_____
_____
_____

Habit Check?
Habit 1:
Habit 2:
Habit 3:
Habit 4:
Daily Self-Motivation
Quote:
Reflection:

Day 18: Growing Your Foundation

Write the one goal from yesterday that would have the "greatest positive impact" on your life right now. This is the goal that if achieved, would help you achieve all other nine goals you identified. This one goal is your "major defining purpose' and drives all future activities.

_____

_____

_____

_____

Write down 20 steps/actions/activities you need to do in order to make your "major defining purpose" goal happen. This is sometimes the hardest step for most people but it's critical in creating a strong foundation for your future. Think hard and make sure you write down 20 things, don't short change yourself.

_____

_____

_____

_____

_____

_____

_____

_____

_____

_____

Habit Check?	
Habit 1:	
Habit 2:	
Habit 3:	
Habit 4:	
Daily Self-Motivation	
Quote:	
Reflection:	

Day 19: Reinforcing Your Foundation

Don't wait until you feel like it. Waiting is the worst thing you can do to your future. Self-disciple is like a muscle. It has to be worked and developed in order for it to be strong. You must make the decision to make this a non-negotiable. Your new life starts today and you will not wait another moment. If you are waiting or have been waiting, why? List at least five areas you could use some personal development and growth. These can be fear, leadership skills, time management, organization, confidence, etc.

_____

_____

_____

_____

Identify at least 5 self-help books that you need to get and read that relate to these areas of personal development. Go to www.amazon.com and search for books, there are a lot of them.

_____

_____

_____

Go buy one of these books immediately. Begin reading every single day. Make this a new daily habit. I get up at least 30 minutes every day before anyone else in my house and read personal development books. I reflect on how it impacts my life. I write in my journal and meditate on how it improves my life. If this sounds silly to you, then you need to look deeper inside you and re-evaluate what's holding you back.

Habit Check?	
Habit 1:	
Habit 2:	
Habit 3:	
Habit 4:	
Daily Self-Motivation	
Quote:	
Reflection:	

Day 20: Accept No Excuses: Daily Challenge #1

Time to test your willpower and self-discipline. For the rest of this week, you are going to challenge yourself with a simple daily challenge. These have to be things that would be a challenge for you but can be completed in one day. For example, give up coffee for one day or don't eat anything with sugar in it for one day. Doable, but not easy.

Daily Challenge #1

_____

_____

_____

What habits are you going to use to make sure you beat this challenge?

_____

_____

_____

_____

_____

Personal Development Reflection

What book are you reading?

_____

What did you learn from it today?

_____

_____

_____

Habit Check?
Habit 1:
Habit 2:
Habit 3:
Habit 4:
Daily Self-Motivation
Quote:
Reflection:

Day 21: Daily Challenge #2

Did you beat yesterday's challenge? Yes or No
How did it make you feel? How can you improve today?

_____
_____
_____
_____

Daily Challenge #2

_____
_____
_____

What habits are you going to use to make sure you beat this challenge?

_____
_____
_____
_____

Personal Development Reflection

What book are you reading?

_____

What did you learn from it today?

_____
_____
_____

Habit Check?
Habit 1:
Habit 2:
Habit 3:
Habit 4:
Daily Self-Motivation
Quote:
Reflection:

Day 22: Daily Challenge #3

Did you beat yesterday's challenge? Yes or No
How did it make you feel? How can you improve today?

_____

_____

_____

_____

Daily Challenge #3

_____

_____

_____

What habits are you going to use to make sure you beat this challenge?

_____

_____

_____

_____

Personal Development Reflection

What book are you reading?

_____

What did you learn from it today?

_____

_____

_____

Habit Check?
Habit 1:
Habit 2:
Habit 3:
Habit 4:
Daily Self-Motivation
Quote:
Reflection:

Day 23: Daily Challenge #4

Did you beat yesterday's challenge? Yes or No
How did it make you feel? How can you improve today?

_____
_____
_____
_____

Daily Challenge #4

_____
_____
_____

What habits are you going to use to make sure you beat this challenge?

_____
_____
_____
_____

Personal Development Reflection

What book are you reading?

_____

What did you learn from it today?

_____
_____
_____

Habit Check?
Habit 1:
Habit 2:
Habit 3:
Habit 4:
Daily Self-Motivation
Quote:
Reflection:

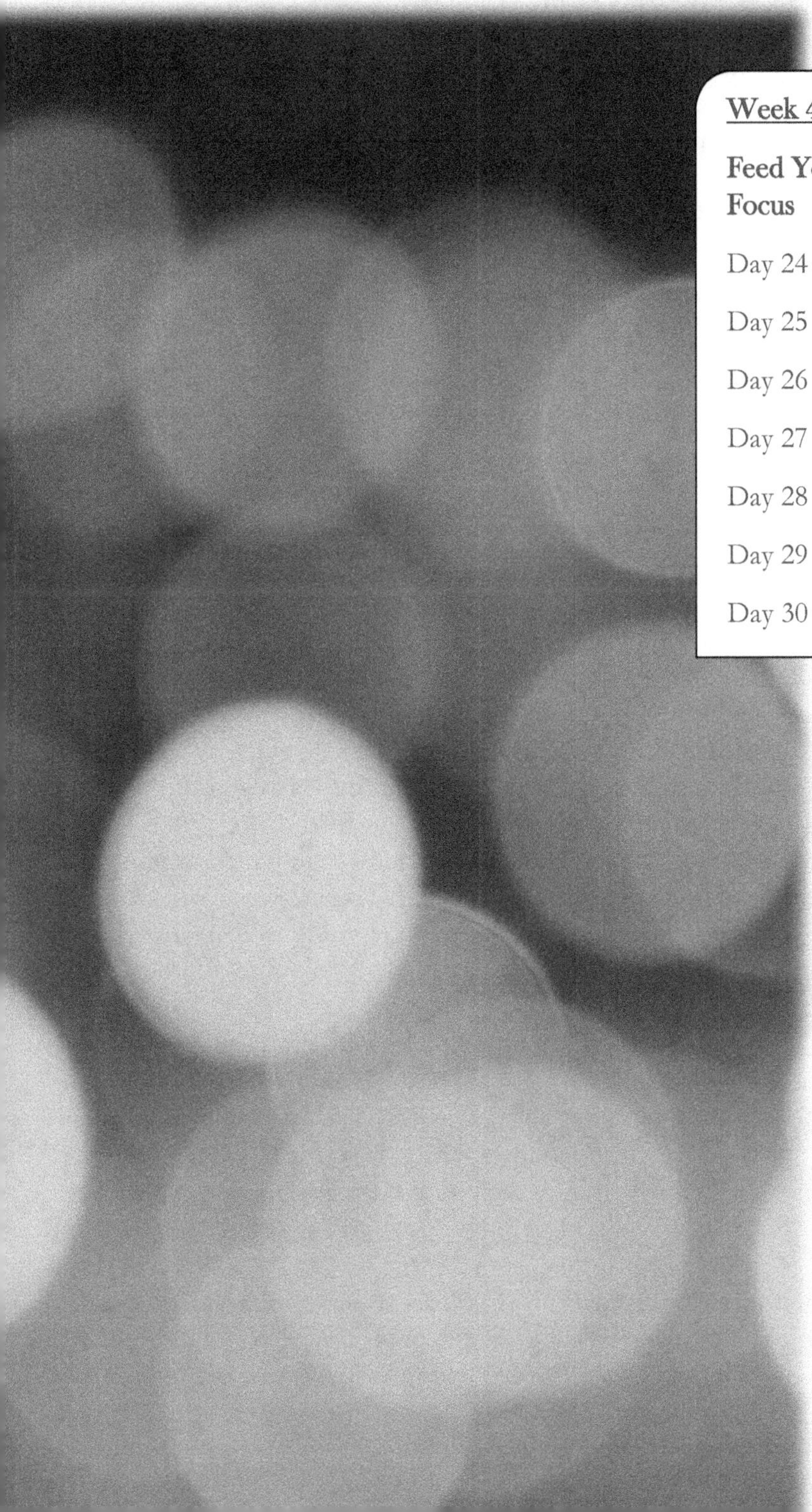

Week 4:

Feed Your Focus

Day 24

Day 25

Day 26

Day 27

Day 28

Day 29

Day 30

Week 4: Feed Your Focus

Time to get real with ourselves. We waste so much time every single day engaging in activities that provide no real benefit to our lives. Sure we may find entertainment value in some of these activities, and while there is value in entertainment it doesn't help us achieve our goals. And if we want to change our lives, we have to reach our goals.

> *"The secret of life, though, is to fall seven times and to get up eight times."*
> — Paulo Coelho

Avoiding distractions is challenging. Distractions are everywhere. Facebook combine with other forms of social media are probably the number one distraction for most people. Just think about how much time you spend each day on Facebook, Instagram, Twitter, or some other new media site that's been developed to suck up all your time. Facebook is so bad it even reminds you to watch the other major time waster called TV.

What are you benefiting from that time? If you are running a business via these social media outlets, that great. But be very careful to not let all the other posts that come up in your news feed distract you. If you have never given this any consideration, then I highly recommend you do it now. Changing your life takes time. If you are wasting too many hours on social media or watching TV, you're going to struggle making real change. It's time to set priorities.

In week 4, you are going to spend some serious time evaluating what you spend your time doing on a daily basis. How many hours do you spend on Facebook or other social media? How many hours do you watch TV a day? Do you play video games, if so for how long? Online shopping? YouTube? Reading? What do you spend most of your time doing?

This is an important evaluation. If you are a person who says "I can't reach my goals because I don't have enough time," you may need to think about giving up one or more of your distractions.

There is always time. Everybody has time. The problem isn't you don't have enough time. The problem is you have to be willing to make time and re-evaluate your priorities. If you want something bad enough, you will make it happen.

And don't worry, we haven't forgotten about those new habits from week 1 or the motivational quotes from week 2 or the personal development from week 3. You will still see those each day this week as well. Are you seeing the pattern here? It takes a strong foundation to create lasting change. And a strong foundation is created though consistency and discipline.

Day 24: Identify Your Distractions
Day 25: Reduce Your Distractions
Day 26: Give Up 1 Distraction
Day 27: Focus on Your Foundation
Day 28: Give Up Another Distraction
Day 29: Make it Routine
Day 30: Change for Life – Repeat

Day 24: Identify Your Distractions

What non work related activities do you engage in every day? (Facebook, Instagram, other social media, surfing the internet, video games, TV, movies, etc.) Write them all down no matter what it is. Monitor your time spent engaging in each of these activities today and write that time down.

_____
_____
_____
_____
_____
_____
_____
_____
_____
_____
_____
_____

Personal Development Reflection

What book are you reading?
_____

What did you learn from it today?
_____
_____
_____

Habit Check?
Habit 1:
Habit 2:
Habit 3:
Habit 4:
Daily Self-Motivation
Quote:
Reflection:

Day 25: Reduce Your Distractions

Consciously make an effort today to reduce the time you spent yesterday on each of your identified distractions. List each distraction down and give yourself a time limit to do each today. Be disciplined and cut the time in half.

_____

_____

_____

_____

_____

_____

_____

_____

_____

_____

_____

_____

Personal Development Reflection

What book are you reading?

_____

What did you learn from it today?

_____

_____

_____

Habit Check?
Habit 1:
Habit 2:
Habit 3:
Habit 4:
Daily Self-Motivation
Quote:
Reflection:

Day 26: Give Up 1 Distraction

Repeat yesterday's limitation on your distractions except take it a step further. Today give up at least one of those distractions completely. Be strong, you can do this.

_____
_____
_____
_____
_____
_____
_____
_____
_____
_____
_____

Personal Development Reflection

What book are you reading?

_____

What did you learn from it today?

_____
_____
_____

Habit Check?
Habit 1:
Habit 2:
Habit 3:
Habit 4:
Daily Self-Motivation
Quote:
Reflection:

Day 27: Focus on Your Foundation

Continue with the limitation on your distractions. Avoid the distraction you gave up. Be strong, you can do this.

_____

_____

_____

_____

_____

Have you been keeping your Major Defining Purpose at the forefront of your mind? What are you doing today to meet your goals?

_____

_____

_____

_____

_____

Personal Development Reflection

What book are you reading?

_____

What did you learn from it today?

_____

_____

_____

Habit Check?
Habit 1:
Habit 2:
Habit 3:
Habit 4:
Daily Self-Motivation
Quote:
Reflection:

Day 28: Give Up Another Distraction

Continue with the limitation on your distractions. Avoid the distraction you gave up. And today, give up a second distraction. Be strong, you can do this.

_____
_____
_____
_____
_____

Major Defining Purpose: What are you doing today to meet your goals?
_____
_____
_____
_____
_____

Personal Development Reflection

What book are you reading?
_____

What did you learn from it today?
_____
_____
_____

Habit Check?
Habit 1:
Habit 2:
Habit 3:
Habit 4:
Daily Self-Motivation
Quote:
Reflection:

Day 29: Make it Routine

Continue with the limitation on your distractions. Avoid both distractions you gave up. Be strong, you can do this.

_____

_____

_____

_____

_____

_____

Major Defining Purpose: What are you doing today to meet your goals?

_____

_____

_____

_____

_____

_____

Personal Development Reflection

What book are you reading?

_____

What did you learn from it today?

_____

_____

_____

Habit Check?
Habit 1:
Habit 2:
Habit 3:
Habit 4:
Daily Self-Motivation
Quote:
Reflection:

Day 30: Change for Life – Repeat

Continue with the limitation on your distractions. Avoid both distractions you gave up. Be strong, you can do this.

_____
_____
_____
_____
_____
_____

Major Defining Purpose: What are you doing today to meet your goals?

_____
_____
_____
_____
_____
_____

Personal Development Reflection

What book are you reading?

_____

What did you learn from it today?

_____
_____
_____

Habit Check?
Habit 1:
Habit 2:
Habit 3:
Habit 4:
Daily Self-Motivation
Quote:
Reflection:

What Next?

Set goals and be consistent…

What Next?

You have learned a tremendous amount over the past four weeks about yourself and about what you truly want out of life. Now it's time to make it stick. You are on a great path to creating permanent good habits that will make you successful. You have mastered self-motivation and personal development. You have learned how to discipline yourself by setting daily challenges and achieving them. Finally, you have reduced your distractions and created time to focus on your goals. You now have what it takes to set big goals, both short-term and long-term, and make them happen.

Use the pages in this section to set yourself up for daily success. Set a few short-term and long-term goals and get to work. You now have the skills to succeed. Included after this section are several entry pages for you to use over the next couple of months. Once you are finished with this book, get a blank journal and start every day with the steps outlined in this section until it becomes a habit you no longer have to think about. It could take three weeks, three months, or over a year. Everybody is different and your rate of creating new habits will be different than the next person. But if you are consistent and disciplined you will succeed.

You are ready for true change.

Setting Goals

Write down the 10 goals you identified on day 17. If they have changed some since then, that's ok. Write them all down.

1._____
2._____
3._____
4._____
5._____
6._____
7._____
8._____
9._____
10._____

Major Defining Purpose?

_____
_____

Set a Deadline to meet this goal: (3 months, 6 months, 1 year)

_____

Write down 20 steps/actions/activities you need to do in order to make your Major Defining Purpose goal happen.

_____
_____
_____
_____
_____
_____
_____
_____
_____
_____
_____
_____
_____
_____
_____

Every Day: Change is Inevitable

Focus on limiting your distractions. Avoid all distractions you have committed to giving up. Be strong, you can do this.

_____
_____
_____
_____
_____
_____

Major Defining Purpose: What are you doing today to meet your goals?

_____
_____
_____
_____
_____

Personal Development Reflection

What book are you reading?

_____

What did you learn from it today?

_____
_____
_____

Habit Check?
Habit 1:
Habit 2:
Habit 3:
Habit 4:
Daily Self-Motivation
Quote:
Reflection:

Repeat

Everyday
hereafter…

Every Day: Change is Inevitable

Focus on limiting your distractions. Avoid all distractions you have committed to giving up. Be strong, you can do this.

_____
_____
_____
_____
_____
_____

Major Defining Purpose: What are you doing today to meet your goals?

_____
_____
_____
_____
_____
_____

Personal Development Reflection

What book are you reading?

_____

What did you learn from it today?

_____
_____
_____

Habit Check?
Habit 1:
Habit 2:
Habit 3:
Habit 4:
Daily Self-Motivation
Quote:
Reflection:

Every Day: Change is Inevitable

Focus on limiting your distractions. Avoid all distractions you have committed to giving up. Be strong, you can do this.

_____
_____
_____
_____
_____
_____

Major Defining Purpose: What are you doing today to meet your goals?

_____
_____
_____
_____
_____
_____

Personal Development Reflection

What book are you reading?

_____

What did you learn from it today?

_____
_____
_____

Habit Check?
Habit 1:
Habit 2:
Habit 3:
Habit 4:
Daily Self-Motivation
Quote:
Reflection:

Every Day: Change is Inevitable

Focus on limiting your distractions. Avoid all distractions you have committed to giving up. Be strong, you can do this.

_____
_____
_____
_____
_____
_____

Major Defining Purpose: What are you doing today to meet your goals?

_____
_____
_____
_____
_____
_____

Personal Development Reflection

What book are you reading?

_____

What did you learn from it today?

_____
_____
_____

Habit Check?
Habit 1:
Habit 2:
Habit 3:
Habit 4:
Daily Self-Motivation
Quote:
Reflection:

Every Day: Change is Inevitable

Focus on limiting your distractions. Avoid all distractions you have committed to giving up. Be strong, you can do this.

_____
_____
_____
_____
_____
_____

Major Defining Purpose: What are you doing today to meet your goals?

_____
_____
_____
_____
_____
_____

Personal Development Reflection

What book are you reading?

_____

What did you learn from it today?

_____
_____
_____

Habit Check?
Habit 1:
Habit 2:
Habit 3:
Habit 4:
Daily Self-Motivation
Quote:
Reflection:

Every Day: Change is Inevitable

Focus on limiting your distractions. Avoid all distractions you have committed to giving up. Be strong, you can do this.

_____
_____
_____
_____
_____
_____

Major Defining Purpose: What are you doing today to meet your goals?

_____
_____
_____
_____
_____
_____

Personal Development Reflection

What book are you reading?

_____

What did you learn from it today?

_____
_____
_____

Habit Check?
Habit 1:
Habit 2:
Habit 3:
Habit 4:
Daily Self-Motivation
Quote:
Reflection:

Every Day: Change is Inevitable

Focus on limiting your distractions. Avoid all distractions you have committed to giving up. Be strong, you can do this.

_____
_____
_____
_____
_____
_____

Major Defining Purpose: What are you doing today to meet your goals?

_____
_____
_____
_____
_____
_____

Personal Development Reflection

What book are you reading?

_____

What did you learn from it today?

_____
_____
_____
_____

Habit Check?
Habit 1:
Habit 2:
Habit 3:
Habit 4:
Daily Self-Motivation
Quote:
Reflection:

Every Day: Change is Inevitable

Focus on limiting your distractions. Avoid all distractions you have committed to giving up. Be strong, you can do this.

_____
_____
_____
_____
_____
_____

Major Defining Purpose: What are you doing today to meet your goals?

_____
_____
_____
_____
_____
_____

Personal Development Reflection

What book are you reading?

_____

What did you learn from it today?

_____
_____
_____

Habit Check?
Habit 1:
Habit 2:
Habit 3:
Habit 4:
Daily Self-Motivation
Quote:
Reflection:

Every Day: Change is Inevitable

Focus on limiting your distractions. Avoid all distractions you have committed to giving up. Be strong, you can do this.

_____
_____
_____
_____
_____
_____

Major Defining Purpose: What are you doing today to meet your goals?

_____
_____
_____
_____
_____
_____

Personal Development Reflection

What book are you reading?

_____

What did you learn from it today?

_____
_____
_____

Habit Check?
Habit 1:
Habit 2:
Habit 3:
Habit 4:
Daily Self-Motivation
Quote:
Reflection:

Every Day: Change is Inevitable

Focus on limiting your distractions. Avoid all distractions you have committed to giving up. Be strong, you can do this.

_____

_____

_____

_____

_____

_____

Major Defining Purpose: What are you doing today to meet your goals?

_____

_____

_____

_____

_____

_____

Personal Development Reflection

What book are you reading?

_____

What did you learn from it today?

_____

_____

_____

Habit Check?
Habit 1:
Habit 2:
Habit 3:
Habit 4:
Daily Self-Motivation
Quote:
Reflection:

Every Day: Change is Inevitable

Focus on limiting your distractions. Avoid all distractions you have committed to giving up. Be strong, you can do this.

_____
_____
_____
_____
_____
_____

Major Defining Purpose: What are you doing today to meet your goals?

_____
_____
_____
_____
_____
_____

Personal Development Reflection

What book are you reading?

_____

What did you learn from it today?

_____
_____
_____

Habit Check?
Habit 1:
Habit 2:
Habit 3:
Habit 4:
Daily Self-Motivation
Quote:
Reflection:

"I have a theory that selflessness and bravery aren't all that different."

— Veronica Roth

Every Day: Change is Inevitable

Focus on limiting your distractions. Avoid all distractions you have committed to giving up. Be strong, you can do this.

_____
_____
_____
_____
_____
_____

Major Defining Purpose: What are you doing today to meet your goals?

_____
_____
_____
_____
_____
_____

Personal Development Reflection

What book are you reading?

_____

What did you learn from it today?

_____
_____
_____

Habit Check?
Habit 1:
Habit 2:
Habit 3:
Habit 4:
Daily Self-Motivation
Quote:
Reflection:

Every Day: Change is Inevitable

Focus on limiting your distractions. Avoid all distractions you have committed to giving up. Be strong, you can do this.

_____
_____
_____
_____
_____
_____

Major Defining Purpose: What are you doing today to meet your goals?

_____
_____
_____
_____
_____
_____

Personal Development Reflection

What book are you reading?

_____

What did you learn from it today?

_____
_____
_____

Habit Check?
Habit 1:
Habit 2:
Habit 3:
Habit 4:
Daily Self-Motivation
Quote:
Reflection:

Every Day: Change is Inevitable

Focus on limiting your distractions. Avoid all distractions you have committed to giving up. Be strong, you can do this.

_____

_____

_____

_____

_____

_____

Major Defining Purpose: What are you doing today to meet your goals?

_____

_____

_____

_____

_____

Personal Development Reflection

What book are you reading?

_____

What did you learn from it today?

_____

_____

_____

Habit Check?
Habit 1:
Habit 2:
Habit 3:
Habit 4:
Daily Self-Motivation
Quote:
Reflection:

Every Day: Change is Inevitable

Focus on limiting your distractions. Avoid all distractions you have committed to giving up. Be strong, you can do this.

_____

_____

_____

_____

_____

_____

Major Defining Purpose: What are you doing today to meet your goals?

_____

_____

_____

_____

_____

Personal Development Reflection

What book are you reading?

_____

What did you learn from it today?

_____

_____

_____

Habit Check?
Habit 1:
Habit 2:
Habit 3:
Habit 4:
Daily Self-Motivation
Quote:
Reflection:

Every Day: Change is Inevitable

Focus on limiting your distractions. Avoid all distractions you have committed to giving up. Be strong, you can do this.

_____

_____

_____

_____

_____

_____

Major Defining Purpose: What are you doing today to meet your goals?

_____

_____

_____

_____

_____

_____

Personal Development Reflection

What book are you reading?

_____

What did you learn from it today?

_____

_____

_____

Habit Check?
Habit 1:
Habit 2:
Habit 3:
Habit 4:
Daily Self-Motivation
Quote:
Reflection:

Every Day: Change is Inevitable

Focus on limiting your distractions. Avoid all distractions you have committed to giving up. Be strong, you can do this.

_____

_____

_____

_____

_____

_____

Major Defining Purpose: What are you doing today to meet your goals?

_____

_____

_____

_____

_____

_____

Personal Development Reflection

What book are you reading?

_____

What did you learn from it today?

_____

_____

_____

Habit Check?
Habit 1:
Habit 2:
Habit 3:
Habit 4:
Daily Self-Motivation
Quote:
Reflection:

Every Day: Change is Inevitable

Focus on limiting your distractions. Avoid all distractions you have committed to giving up. Be strong, you can do this.

_____
_____
_____
_____
_____
_____

Major Defining Purpose: What are you doing today to meet your goals?

_____
_____
_____
_____
_____

Personal Development Reflection

What book are you reading?

_____

What did you learn from it today?

_____
_____
_____

Habit Check?
Habit 1:
Habit 2:
Habit 3:
Habit 4:
Daily Self-Motivation
Quote:
Reflection:

Every Day: Change is Inevitable

Focus on limiting your distractions. Avoid all distractions you have committed to giving up. Be strong, you can do this.

_____
_____
_____
_____
_____
_____

Major Defining Purpose: What are you doing today to meet your goals?

_____
_____
_____
_____
_____
_____

Personal Development Reflection

What book are you reading?

_____

What did you learn from it today?

_____
_____
_____

Habit Check?
Habit 1:
Habit 2:
Habit 3:
Habit 4:
Daily Self-Motivation
Quote:
Reflection:

Every Day: Change is Inevitable

Focus on limiting your distractions. Avoid all distractions you have committed to giving up. Be strong, you can do this.

_____
_____
_____
_____
_____
_____

Major Defining Purpose: What are you doing today to meet your goals?

_____
_____
_____
_____
_____
_____

Personal Development Reflection

What book are you reading?

_____

What did you learn from it today?

_____
_____
_____

Habit Check?
Habit 1:
Habit 2:
Habit 3:
Habit 4:
Daily Self-Motivation
Quote:
Reflection:

Every Day: Change is Inevitable

Focus on limiting your distractions. Avoid all distractions you have committed to giving up. Be strong, you can do this.

_____

_____

_____

_____

_____

_____

Major Defining Purpose: What are you doing today to meet your goals?

_____

_____

_____

_____

_____

Personal Development Reflection

What book are you reading?

_____

What did you learn from it today?

_____

_____

_____

Habit Check?
Habit 1:
Habit 2:
Habit 3:
Habit 4:
Daily Self-Motivation
Quote:
Reflection:

"Laughter is timeless. Imagination has no age. And dreams are forever."
— Walt Disney Company

Every Day: Change is Inevitable

Focus on limiting your distractions. Avoid all distractions you have committed to giving up. Be strong, you can do this.

_____
_____
_____
_____
_____
_____

Major Defining Purpose: What are you doing today to meet your goals?

_____
_____
_____
_____
_____
_____

Personal Development Reflection

What book are you reading?

_____

What did you learn from it today?

_____
_____
_____

Habit Check?
Habit 1:
Habit 2:
Habit 3:
Habit 4:
Daily Self-Motivation
Quote:
Reflection:

Every Day: Change is Inevitable

Focus on limiting your distractions. Avoid all distractions you have committed to giving up. Be strong, you can do this.

_____
_____
_____
_____
_____
_____

Major Defining Purpose: What are you doing today to meet your goals?

_____
_____
_____
_____
_____
_____

Personal Development Reflection

What book are you reading?

_____

What did you learn from it today?

_____
_____
_____

Habit Check?
Habit 1:
Habit 2:
Habit 3:
Habit 4:
Daily Self-Motivation
Quote:
Reflection:

Every Day: Change is Inevitable

Focus on limiting your distractions. Avoid all distractions you have committed to giving up. Be strong, you can do this.

_____
_____
_____
_____
_____
_____

Major Defining Purpose: What are you doing today to meet your goals?

_____
_____
_____
_____
_____
_____

Personal Development Reflection

What book are you reading?

_____

What did you learn from it today?

_____
_____
_____

Habit Check?
Habit 1:
Habit 2:
Habit 3:
Habit 4:
Daily Self-Motivation
Quote:
Reflection:

Every Day: Change is Inevitable

Focus on limiting your distractions. Avoid all distractions you have committed to giving up. Be strong, you can do this.

_____

_____

_____

_____

_____

_____

Major Defining Purpose: What are you doing today to meet your goals?

_____

_____

_____

_____

_____

_____

Personal Development Reflection

What book are you reading?

_____

What did you learn from it today?

_____

_____

_____

Habit Check?	
Habit 1:	
Habit 2:	
Habit 3:	
Habit 4:	
Daily Self-Motivation	
Quote:	
Reflection:	

Every Day: Change is Inevitable

Focus on limiting your distractions. Avoid all distractions you have committed to giving up. Be strong, you can do this.

_____
_____
_____
_____
_____
_____

Major Defining Purpose: What are you doing today to meet your goals?

_____
_____
_____
_____
_____

Personal Development Reflection

What book are you reading?

_____

What did you learn from it today?

_____
_____
_____

Habit Check?
Habit 1:
Habit 2:
Habit 3:
Habit 4:
Daily Self-Motivation
Quote:
Reflection:

Every Day: Change is Inevitable

Focus on limiting your distractions. Avoid all distractions you have committed to giving up. Be strong, you can do this.

_____

_____

_____

_____

_____

_____

Major Defining Purpose: What are you doing today to meet your goals?

_____

_____

_____

_____

_____

_____

Personal Development Reflection

What book are you reading?

_____

What did you learn from it today?

_____

_____

_____

Habit Check?
Habit 1:
Habit 2:
Habit 3:
Habit 4:
Daily Self-Motivation
Quote:
Reflection:

Every Day: Change is Inevitable

Focus on limiting your distractions. Avoid all distractions you have committed to giving up. Be strong, you can do this.

_____
_____
_____
_____
_____
_____

Major Defining Purpose: What are you doing today to meet your goals?

_____
_____
_____
_____
_____
_____

Personal Development Reflection

What book are you reading?

_____

What did you learn from it today?

_____
_____
_____

Habit Check?
Habit 1:
Habit 2:
Habit 3:
Habit 4:
Daily Self-Motivation
Quote:
Reflection:

Every Day: Change is Inevitable

Focus on limiting your distractions. Avoid all distractions you have committed to giving up. Be strong, you can do this.

_____

_____

_____

_____

_____

_____

Major Defining Purpose: What are you doing today to meet your goals?

_____

_____

_____

_____

_____

_____

Personal Development Reflection

What book are you reading?

_____

What did you learn from it today?

_____

_____

_____

Habit Check?
Habit 1:
Habit 2:
Habit 3:
Habit 4:
Daily Self-Motivation
Quote:
Reflection:

Every Day: Change is Inevitable

Focus on limiting your distractions. Avoid all distractions you have committed to giving up. Be strong, you can do this.

_____
_____
_____
_____
_____
_____

Major Defining Purpose: What are you doing today to meet your goals?

_____
_____
_____
_____
_____
_____

Personal Development Reflection

What book are you reading?

_____

What did you learn from it today?

_____
_____
_____

Habit Check?
Habit 1:
Habit 2:
Habit 3:
Habit 4:
Daily Self-Motivation
Quote:
Reflection:

*"Do not go where the path may lead, go instead where there is no path
and leave a trail."*
— Ralph Waldo Emerson

Every Day: Change is Inevitable

Focus on limiting your distractions. Avoid all distractions you have committed to giving up. Be strong, you can do this.

_____
_____
_____
_____
_____
_____

Major Defining Purpose: What are you doing today to meet your goals?

_____
_____
_____
_____
_____

Personal Development Reflection

What book are you reading?

_____

What did you learn from it today?

_____
_____
_____

Habit Check?
Habit 1:
Habit 2:
Habit 3:
Habit 4:
Daily Self-Motivation
Quote:
Reflection:

Every Day: Change is Inevitable

Focus on limiting your distractions. Avoid all distractions you have committed to giving up. Be strong, you can do this.

_____

_____

_____

_____

_____

Major Defining Purpose: What are you doing today to meet your goals?

_____

_____

_____

_____

_____

Personal Development Reflection

What book are you reading?

_____

What did you learn from it today?

_____

_____

_____

Habit Check?
Habit 1:
Habit 2:
Habit 3:
Habit 4:
Daily Self-Motivation
Quote:
Reflection:

Every Day: Change is Inevitable

Focus on limiting your distractions. Avoid all distractions you have committed to giving up. Be strong, you can do this.

_____
_____
_____
_____
_____
_____

Major Defining Purpose: What are you doing today to meet your goals?

_____
_____
_____
_____
_____
_____

Personal Development Reflection

What book are you reading?

_____

What did you learn from it today?

_____
_____
_____
_____

Habit Check?		
Habit 1:		
Habit 2:		
Habit 3:		
Habit 4:		
Daily Self-Motivation		
Quote:		
Reflection:		

Every Day: Change is Inevitable

Focus on limiting your distractions. Avoid all distractions you have committed to giving up. Be strong, you can do this.

_____

_____

_____

_____

_____

_____

Major Defining Purpose: What are you doing today to meet your goals?

_____

_____

_____

_____

_____

_____

Personal Development Reflection

What book are you reading?

_____

What did you learn from it today?

_____

_____

_____

Habit Check?
Habit 1:
Habit 2:
Habit 3:
Habit 4:
Daily Self-Motivation
Quote:
Reflection:

Every Day: Change is Inevitable

Focus on limiting your distractions. Avoid all distractions you have committed to giving up. Be strong, you can do this.

Major Defining Purpose: What are you doing today to meet your goals?

Personal Development Reflection

What book are you reading?

What did you learn from it today?

Habit Check?
Habit 1:
Habit 2:
Habit 3:
Habit 4:
Daily Self-Motivation
Quote:
Reflection:

Every Day: Change is Inevitable

Focus on limiting your distractions. Avoid all distractions you have committed to giving up. Be strong, you can do this.

_____

_____

_____

_____

_____

_____

Major Defining Purpose: What are you doing today to meet your goals?

_____

_____

_____

_____

_____

_____

Personal Development Reflection

What book are you reading?

_____

What did you learn from it today?

_____

_____

_____

Habit Check?
Habit 1:
Habit 2:
Habit 3:
Habit 4:
Daily Self-Motivation
Quote:
Reflection:

Every Day: Change is Inevitable

Focus on limiting your distractions. Avoid all distractions you have committed to giving up. Be strong, you can do this.

_____
_____
_____
_____
_____
_____

Major Defining Purpose: What are you doing today to meet your goals?

_____
_____
_____
_____
_____
_____

Personal Development Reflection

What book are you reading?

_____

What did you learn from it today?

_____
_____
_____

Habit Check?
Habit 1:
Habit 2:
Habit 3:
Habit 4:
Daily Self-Motivation
Quote:
Reflection:

Every Day: Change is Inevitable

Focus on limiting your distractions. Avoid all distractions you have committed to giving up. Be strong, you can do this.

_____
_____
_____
_____
_____
_____

Major Defining Purpose: What are you doing today to meet your goals?

_____
_____
_____
_____
_____
_____

Personal Development Reflection

What book are you reading?

_____

What did you learn from it today?

_____
_____
_____

Habit Check?
Habit 1:
Habit 2:
Habit 3:
Habit 4:
Daily Self-Motivation
Quote:
Reflection:

Every Day: Change is Inevitable

Focus on limiting your distractions. Avoid all distractions you have committed to giving up. Be strong, you can do this.

_____

_____

_____

_____

_____

_____

Major Defining Purpose: What are you doing today to meet your goals?

_____

_____

_____

_____

_____

Personal Development Reflection

What book are you reading?

_____

What did you learn from it today?

_____

_____

_____

Habit Check?
Habit 1:
Habit 2:
Habit 3:
Habit 4:
Daily Self-Motivation
Quote:
Reflection:

Every Day: Change is Inevitable

Focus on limiting your distractions. Avoid all distractions you have committed to giving up. Be strong, you can do this.

_____

_____

_____

_____

_____

Major Defining Purpose: What are you doing today to meet your goals?

_____

_____

_____

_____

_____

Personal Development Reflection

What book are you reading?

_____

What did you learn from it today?

_____

_____

_____

Habit Check?
Habit 1:
Habit 2:
Habit 3:
Habit 4:
Daily Self-Motivation
Quote:
Reflection:

"The mind is its own place, and in itself can make a heaven of hell, a hell of heaven."
— John Milton

Every Day: Change is Inevitable

Focus on limiting your distractions. Avoid all distractions you have committed to giving up. Be strong, you can do this.

_____

_____

_____

_____

_____

Major Defining Purpose: What are you doing today to meet your goals?

_____

_____

_____

_____

_____

Personal Development Reflection

What book are you reading?

_____

What did you learn from it today?

_____

_____

_____

Habit Check?
Habit 1:
Habit 2:
Habit 3:
Habit 4:
Daily Self-Motivation
Quote:
Reflection:

Every Day: Change is Inevitable

Focus on limiting your distractions. Avoid all distractions you have committed to giving up. Be strong, you can do this.

_____
_____
_____
_____
_____
_____

Major Defining Purpose: What are you doing today to meet your goals?

_____
_____
_____
_____
_____
_____

Personal Development Reflection

What book are you reading?

_____

What did you learn from it today?

_____
_____
_____

Habit Check?
Habit 1:
Habit 2:
Habit 3:
Habit 4:
Daily Self-Motivation
Quote:
Reflection:

Every Day: Change is Inevitable

Focus on limiting your distractions. Avoid all distractions you have committed to giving up. Be strong, you can do this.

_____

_____

_____

_____

_____

_____

Major Defining Purpose: What are you doing today to meet your goals?

_____

_____

_____

_____

_____

Personal Development Reflection

What book are you reading?

_____

What did you learn from it today?

_____

_____

_____

Habit Check?
Habit 1:
Habit 2:
Habit 3:
Habit 4:
Daily Self-Motivation
Quote:
Reflection:

Every Day: Change is Inevitable

Focus on limiting your distractions. Avoid all distractions you have committed to giving up. Be strong, you can do this.

_____
_____
_____
_____
_____
_____

Major Defining Purpose: What are you doing today to meet your goals?

_____
_____
_____
_____
_____
_____

Personal Development Reflection

What book are you reading?

_____

What did you learn from it today?

_____
_____
_____

Habit Check?
Habit 1:
Habit 2:
Habit 3:
Habit 4:
Daily Self-Motivation
Quote:
Reflection:

Every Day: Change is Inevitable

Focus on limiting your distractions. Avoid all distractions you have committed to giving up. Be strong, you can do this.

_____

_____

_____

_____

_____

_____

Major Defining Purpose: What are you doing today to meet your goals?

_____

_____

_____

_____

_____

Personal Development Reflection

What book are you reading?

_____

What did you learn from it today?

_____

_____

_____

Habit Check?
Habit 1:
Habit 2:
Habit 3:
Habit 4:
Daily Self-Motivation
Quote:
Reflection:

Every Day: Change is Inevitable

Focus on limiting your distractions. Avoid all distractions you have committed to giving up. Be strong, you can do this.

_____
_____
_____
_____
_____
_____

Major Defining Purpose: What are you doing today to meet your goals?

_____
_____
_____
_____
_____
_____

Personal Development Reflection

What book are you reading?

_____

What did you learn from it today?

_____
_____
_____

Habit Check?
Habit 1:
Habit 2:
Habit 3:
Habit 4:
Daily Self-Motivation
Quote:
Reflection:

Every Day: Change is Inevitable

Focus on limiting your distractions. Avoid all distractions you have committed to giving up. Be strong, you can do this.

_____
_____
_____
_____
_____
_____

Major Defining Purpose: What are you doing today to meet your goals?

_____
_____
_____
_____
_____
_____

Personal Development Reflection

What book are you reading?

_____

What did you learn from it today?

_____
_____
_____

Habit Check?
Habit 1:
Habit 2:
Habit 3:
Habit 4:
Daily Self-Motivation
Quote:
Reflection:

Every Day: Change is Inevitable

Focus on limiting your distractions. Avoid all distractions you have committed to giving up. Be strong, you can do this.

_____
_____
_____
_____
_____
_____

Major Defining Purpose: What are you doing today to meet your goals?

_____
_____
_____
_____
_____
_____

Personal Development Reflection

What book are you reading?

_____

What did you learn from it today?

_____
_____
_____

Habit Check?
Habit 1:
Habit 2:
Habit 3:
Habit 4:
Daily Self-Motivation
Quote:
Reflection:

Every Day: Change is Inevitable

Focus on limiting your distractions. Avoid all distractions you have committed to giving up. Be strong, you can do this.

_____

_____

_____

_____

_____

_____

Major Defining Purpose: What are you doing today to meet your goals?

_____

_____

_____

_____

_____

Personal Development Reflection

What book are you reading?

_____

What did you learn from it today?

_____

_____

_____

Habit Check?
Habit 1:
Habit 2:
Habit 3:
Habit 4:
Daily Self-Motivation
Quote:
Reflection:

"Worse than not realizing the dreams of your youth would be to have been young and never dreamed at all."

— Jean Genet

Every Day: Change is Inevitable

Focus on limiting your distractions. Avoid all distractions you have committed to giving up. Be strong, you can do this.

_____

_____

_____

_____

_____

_____

Major Defining Purpose: What are you doing today to meet your goals?

_____

_____

_____

_____

_____

Personal Development Reflection

What book are you reading?

_____

What did you learn from it today?

_____

_____

_____

Habit Check?
Habit 1:
Habit 2:
Habit 3:
Habit 4:
Daily Self-Motivation
Quote:
Reflection:

Every Day: Change is Inevitable

Focus on limiting your distractions. Avoid all distractions you have committed to giving up. Be strong, you can do this.

_____

_____

_____

_____

_____

_____

Major Defining Purpose: What are you doing today to meet your goals?

_____

_____

_____

_____

_____

_____

Personal Development Reflection

What book are you reading?

_____

What did you learn from it today?

_____

_____

_____

Habit Check?
Habit 1:
Habit 2:
Habit 3:
Habit 4:
Daily Self-Motivation
Quote:
Reflection:

Every Day: Change is Inevitable

Focus on limiting your distractions. Avoid all distractions you have committed to giving up. Be strong, you can do this.

_____
_____
_____
_____
_____
_____

Major Defining Purpose: What are you doing today to meet your goals?

_____
_____
_____
_____
_____

Personal Development Reflection

What book are you reading?

_____

What did you learn from it today?

_____
_____
_____

Habit Check?
Habit 1:
Habit 2:
Habit 3:
Habit 4:
Daily Self-Motivation
Quote:
Reflection:

Every Day: Change is Inevitable

Focus on limiting your distractions. Avoid all distractions you have committed to giving up. Be strong, you can do this.

_____

_____

_____

_____

_____

_____

Major Defining Purpose: What are you doing today to meet your goals?

_____

_____

_____

_____

_____

_____

Personal Development Reflection

What book are you reading?

_____

What did you learn from it today?

_____

_____

_____

Habit Check?
Habit 1:
Habit 2:
Habit 3:
Habit 4:
Daily Self-Motivation
Quote:
Reflection:

Every Day: Change is Inevitable

Focus on limiting your distractions. Avoid all distractions you have committed to giving up. Be strong, you can do this.

_____
_____
_____
_____
_____
_____

Major Defining Purpose: What are you doing today to meet your goals?

_____
_____
_____
_____
_____

Personal Development Reflection

What book are you reading?

_____

What did you learn from it today?

_____
_____
_____

Habit Check?
Habit 1:
Habit 2:
Habit 3:
Habit 4:
Daily Self-Motivation
Quote:
Reflection:

Every Day: Change is Inevitable

Focus on limiting your distractions. Avoid all distractions you have committed to giving up. Be strong, you can do this.

_____

_____

_____

_____

_____

_____

Major Defining Purpose: What are you doing today to meet your goals?

_____

_____

_____

_____

_____

Personal Development Reflection

What book are you reading?

_____

What did you learn from it today?

_____

_____

_____

Habit Check?
Habit 1:
Habit 2:
Habit 3:
Habit 4:
Daily Self-Motivation
Quote:
Reflection:

Every Day: Change is Inevitable

Focus on limiting your distractions. Avoid all distractions you have committed to giving up. Be strong, you can do this.

_____

_____

_____

_____

_____

_____

Major Defining Purpose: What are you doing today to meet your goals?

_____

_____

_____

_____

_____

_____

Personal Development Reflection

What book are you reading?

_____

What did you learn from it today?

_____

_____

_____

Habit Check?
Habit 1:
Habit 2:
Habit 3:
Habit 4:
Daily Self-Motivation
Quote:
Reflection:

Every Day: Change is Inevitable

Focus on limiting your distractions. Avoid all distractions you have committed to giving up. Be strong, you can do this.

_____
_____
_____
_____
_____
_____

Major Defining Purpose: What are you doing today to meet your goals?

_____
_____
_____
_____
_____
_____

Personal Development Reflection

What book are you reading?

_____

What did you learn from it today?

_____
_____
_____

Habit Check?

Habit 1:

Habit 2:

Habit 3:

Habit 4:

Daily Self-Motivation

Quote:

Reflection:

Every Day: Change is Inevitable

Focus on limiting your distractions. Avoid all distractions you have committed to giving up. Be strong, you can do this.

_____
_____
_____
_____
_____
_____

Major Defining Purpose: What are you doing today to meet your goals?

_____
_____
_____
_____
_____
_____

Personal Development Reflection

What book are you reading?

_____

What did you learn from it today?

_____
_____
_____

Habit Check?
Habit 1:
Habit 2:
Habit 3:
Habit 4:
Daily Self-Motivation
Quote:
Reflection:

Every Day: Change is Inevitable

Focus on limiting your distractions. Avoid all distractions you have committed to giving up. Be strong, you can do this.

_____
_____
_____
_____
_____
_____

Major Defining Purpose: What are you doing today to meet your goals?

_____
_____
_____
_____
_____
_____

Personal Development Reflection

What book are you reading?

_____

What did you learn from it today?

_____
_____
_____

Habit Check?
Habit 1:
Habit 2:
Habit 3:
Habit 4:
Daily Self-Motivation
Quote:
Reflection:

Every Day: Change is Inevitable

Focus on limiting your distractions. Avoid all distractions you have committed to giving up. Be strong, you can do this.

_____
_____
_____
_____
_____
_____

Major Defining Purpose: What are you doing today to meet your goals?

_____
_____
_____
_____
_____

Personal Development Reflection

What book are you reading?

_____

What did you learn from it today?

_____
_____
_____

Habit Check?
Habit 1:
Habit 2:
Habit 3:
Habit 4:
Daily Self-Motivation
Quote:
Reflection:

Every Day: Change is Inevitable

Focus on limiting your distractions. Avoid all distractions you have committed to giving up. Be strong, you can do this.

_____

_____

_____

_____

_____

_____

Major Defining Purpose: What are you doing today to meet your goals?

_____

_____

_____

_____

_____

_____

Personal Development Reflection

What book are you reading?

_____

What did you learn from it today?

_____

_____

_____

Habit Check?	
Habit 1:	
Habit 2:	
Habit 3:	
Habit 4:	
Daily Self-Motivation	
Quote:	
Reflection:	

Every Day: Change is Inevitable

Focus on limiting your distractions. Avoid all distractions you have committed to giving up. Be strong, you can do this.

_____

_____

_____

_____

_____

_____

Major Defining Purpose: What are you doing today to meet your goals?

_____

_____

_____

_____

_____

Personal Development Reflection

What book are you reading?

_____

What did you learn from it today?

_____

_____

_____

Habit Check?
Habit 1:
Habit 2:
Habit 3:
Habit 4:
Daily Self-Motivation
Quote:
Reflection:

FREE DOWNLOAD

Get a FREE printable pdf companion book.

Guided Motivation: Guidebook for Self-Reflection, Journal Your way to Success and Happiness is the perfect companion for this book.

Sign up for author's New Releases mailing list and get a FREE companion workbook.

Click here to get started: http://eepurl.com/bRBdhb

About the Author

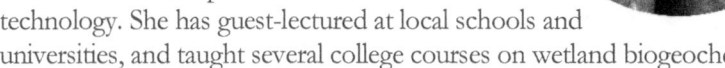

Dr. Angelique Bochnak is an accomplished writer, author, and speaker. Angelique has authored or co-authored numerous well-received technical reports, including published peer-reviewed journal articles. She is often invited to speak at national and local conferences on topics related to her research in ecosystem restoration and empowering women in leadership roles in science and technology. She has guest-lectured at local schools and universities, and taught several college courses on wetland biogeochemistry, soil science and environmental and biological sciences.

Much of Angelique's writing is focused on empowering woman to embrace leadership and reach their life goals. More often than not, Angelique has found herself to be the only female professional on her team. With no mentor to learn from and no other women to model herself after, she was left learning how to maneuver through her career by trial and error. After a lot of mistakes and a few successes, she was able to achieve the level of success she desired. Her writing not only shares her experiences but also provides valuable resources to women everywhere who also desire to achieve success in their careers.

Angelique has authored two non-fiction books. She is expected to release two more non-fiction books in 2016. Angelique is also working on her first fiction novel.

Join my mailing list for updates on upcoming books (and the occasional free publication).

Click here to join: http://eepurl.com/bRLrx5

Connect with Me:
Facebook: www.facebook.com/angeliquebochnak/
Instagram: www.instagram.com/angeliquebochnak/
Twitter: www.twitter.com/AMKBochnak
Goodreads: www.goodreads.com/angeliquebochnak
Blog: www.angeliquebochnak.com/blog/
Website: www.angeliquebochnak.com/

www.ingramcontent.com/pod-product-compliance
Lightning Source LLC
Chambersburg PA
CBHW070322190526
45169CB00005B/1710